TOO LIKE THE LIGHTNING

PROSE POEMS TO MY ALMOST LOVES

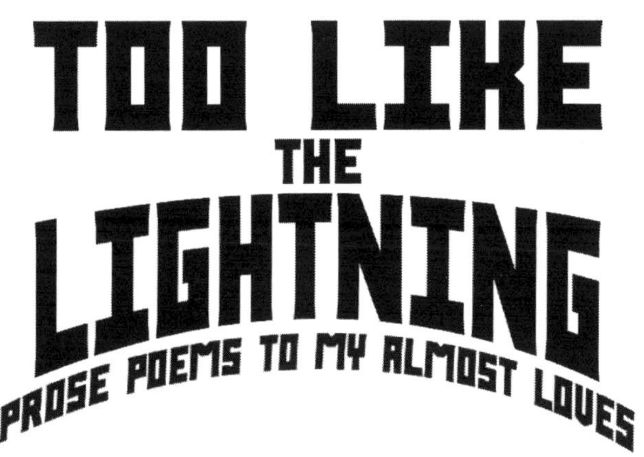

BY TERESA SPENCER
ILLUSTRATED BY SYDNEY SCHWINDT

Washington, DC

Taffety Punk Theatre Company
545 7th Street SE
Washington, DC 20003
www.taffetypunk.com

Library of Congress Control Number: 2024905764
ISBN: 978-1-7329571-1-4 (paperback)
ISBN: 978-1-7329571-2-1 (audiobook)
Taffety Punk #59

Interior design: Creative Publishing Book Design
Publishing consultant: Redwood Publishing, LLC
Taffety Punk Logo by Ryan Carroll Nelson © 2024

NOTE: The prose poems in this collection are based on factual encounters, with large and small embellishments added by the author for giggles. Any identifying information about the people who lived these encounters has been changed, for their privacy and sanity.

10 9 8 7 6 5 4 3 2 1

I have no joy of this contract tonight.
It is too rash, too unadvised, too sudden,
Too like the lightning, which doth cease to be
Ere one can say 'It lightens.'

— Juliet, *Romeo and Juliet*, William Shakespeare

Men are afraid women will laugh at them.
Women are afraid men will kill them.

— Margaret Atwood

Contents

About *Too Like the Lightning*

I was driving on Route 50 outside DC a few years ago, and a trucker blew his air horn at me and waggled his first two fingers—and his tongue—as he gunned by. You know the gesture. Like an NC-17 peace sign.

I went through a gymnastics routine of feelings in maybe 2.5 seconds that's all-too-familiar to women. First, there was a jolt of real adrenaline and fear because air horns are loud and we were all going 70 mph, and nobody in a Honda wants to have any kind of intimate exchange with a semi. And then there was this total revulsion, like did that guy really just make *that* gesture? But close on the heels was shame. What did I do to invite it? I have this habit of pulling my left leg up on the seat when I'm on a long drive. Did he see my knee poking up by the window and think, "Ooh, she wants it"? My shameful, shameful, denim-clad knee?

Dudes who do this—who interrupt and sexualize women in public space—want to provoke exactly that kind of discomfort. That fear and embarrassment. It wasn't so much that the trucker was getting his rocks off on seeing my knee inside my jeans, it was that he was getting his rocks off on feeling some small degree of power over me. Street harassment lives, in a very real way, on the same spectrum of behaviors as sexual harassment in the workplace and even sexual assault. It's about control, and it's about reinforcement of male dominance.

But if you try to point out that dynamic, people—both street harassers and their apologists—will come back at you with a whole host of reasons why you're overreacting. My favorite of these apologies is, "It's only a compliment!" This is a pretty deft gaslight. Now, not only am I overreacting for feeling exactly the fear and embarrassment the street harasser *wants* me to feel—but I'm also ungrateful. Damn. A girl could drive herself crazy trying to accommodate these contradictory demands.

So I decided that instead of trying to refute the street harasser's ass-backwards logic, I'd just meet him where he is. He's complimenting me? He's an innocent sweetheart just trying to meet a lady? Okay! If that very special brand of peace sign was just his misguided, ham-fisted conversation starter, then let's have a conversation. Like, what if we went out for coffee? Would we talk about the books we're reading? Share our little devastations, our little triumphs?

I wrote him a love poem about our future together. And then I put it on the internet.

Juliet worries that her love-at-first-sight for Romeo will end up "Too like the lightning, which doth cease to be ere one can say 'It lightens.'" Isn't that exactly how things are between dudes hollering about butts on the street and women who are just trying to exist in public space? They're these tragic little missed connections. So I called this collection *Too Like the Lightning: Prose Poems to My Almost Loves*.

When I first started making fun of perverts on the internet, I had a list of five or six standout street harassment moments from my own life that I thought would make good love poems. But before I had even gotten through the list, women and people of marginalized gender identities started sending me their stories. Pretty soon, I had a list of poems to write that was longer than I could keep up with. And I began to find that the street context is secondary. The point for harassers is to put women in their place in public. That might include catcalling, yes, but also mansplaining, online harassment, and sometimes the more sinister behaviors—when the threat of sexual violence is overt, not just implied: following, groping, assault.

Eventually, I found that the hyper-romantic prose poem form (as much as it makes me giggle) was secondary too. I threw in some other forms, from fiction to online customer review, as my best attempts to capture the kernels of insight I was hearing. With the exception of *Menelaus and the Fake Helen*, all of the pieces in this collection are based on the lived experiences people have been willing to share with me. And even *Menelaus and the Fake Helen* is based on an actual version of the myth that, I imagine, some ancient Greek guys once found kind of titillating.

For folks who don't routinely find themselves exposed or targeted in this specific way, I offer this collection as an opportunity to step into an experience that you might only rarely hear about and less rarely witness. A thing that all women know anecdotally, and that researchers are starting to systematically uncover (please check out the list of resources at the end of this introduction!), is that many harassers only harass when there is no one else around, or only harass in covert ways that bystanders, especially male bystanders, might not even notice. If this isn't a tacit admission that they know what they're doing is wrong, I don't know what is. But it also makes it really tough for men, who are more rarely the targets of this kind of behavior, to realize the scope of the problem and the severity of its consequences. The reality is that while most men don't sexually harass strangers in public places, most people who *do* sexually harass strangers in public places are men. So I hope this is of interest to good dudes because it's an opportunity not only to understand an experience that severely negatively impacts your friends, lovers, partners, colleagues, and family members on a relentless basis, but it also gets in the way of you, a good dude, just being a human living your non-harming life.

To those for whom these moments of verbal, psychological, and even physical violence are routine, these are really my love poems to you. I see you. Harassers do this shit to make us small. To make us feel that our voices, our very presence, are unwelcome in the public sphere. I want us all to feel as big and as full and as human as we actually are.

— Teresa Spencer

Resources

Below are some resources that I've found helpful. These are places where you can share your story, better understand gender-based harassment as a social phenomenon in our world, or get help coping:

Stop Street Harassment

stopstreetharassment.org

This organization works worldwide to end gender-based street harassment. If the anecdotes in *Too Like the Lightning* don't convince you, click the "Statistics" link under "Resources" on this website and be alarmed.

National Street Harassment Hotline, run by Stop Street Harassment

Available between 12 p.m. and 12 a.m. ET, toll-free, English and Spanish: 855-897-5910

You can also access the hotline by anonymous IM chat at the Stop Street Harassment website above under "Help & Advice."

Receive support for coping with street harassment as well as advice on how to respond and information about your legal rights.

Right To Be
righttobe.org

This organization documents instances of street harassment for research and consciousness-raising and provides bystander intervention training.

HeartMob, run by Right To Be
iheartmob.org

If you've experienced online harassment, this community will document your story on its secure platform and offer messages of support and assistance if you wish to report it to the social media platform where the harassment occurred.

Safecity, run by Red Dot Foundation
safecity.in

This app/platform crowdsources personal stories of sexual harassment in public spaces.

Stand Up
standup-international.com

A training program designed to help prevent street harassment and build safe, inclusive spaces for all. You can take the ten-minute online training yourself or book their experts to come to your event or organization.

Too Like the Lightning

Prose Poems to My Almost Loves

To the Trucker

A prose poem to the trucker who blasts his air horn at women as he passes on the right, making them startle—and twist 'round—and wonder: Are my brights on?

No. It's a blue midmorning, and I'm pretty sure I see your fingers waggling suggestively in the rearview as you pull away, leaving me with only a memory, a hairy patch of elbow jutting from the driver's side window. A whisper of exhaust. Our connection—so fleeting. Your come-on—so appealing. What is your number? How do I date you? I see you sanding the wooden rungs of our children's treehouse ladder, driving me in the cab of your big rig to my colonoscopies, holding my paper-thin wrist in your flat, chappy palm as I slip—cherished, beloved—from this world. Another love lost to the dotted yellow line disappearing over the horizon.

To the Shouter

A prose poem to the street harasser who just turns up the volume.

"How you doin' tonight?" you ask me, sotto voce. And then again, still in dulcet tones but with rising fervor: "How you DOIN' tonight?" And, finally, a third time, your throaty baritone ricocheting off the night air: "HOW YOU DOIN' TONIGHT?" I like that you understand passion and volume to be equivalent. You're obviously a subtle man, delicate in sensibilities, refined in delivery. Might you and I continue the conversation? Let's scream sweet nothings right into each other's faces. I want to roll over in the morning to discover your warm body swathed in a tangle of bedsheets and dappled sunlight and shout "GOOD MORNING, LOVER!" into your tender eardrum. I want to grow old with you, accumulating noise complaints and early-onset hearing loss. Someday, when we are frail and gray, my love for you will rest gently in the simple exchanges between us. "Baby, it's your brother on the phone . . . No, I KNOW your mother's dead, it's your BROTHER. Just pick up. JUST PICK UP THE PHONE." God, I burn for you.

#
THE NEW BABY-SITTERS CLUB
#1
MARY ANNE AND TOO MANY BOYS
TAFFETYPUNK

To the Childcare Specialists

A prose poem to the group of drunk guys who catcalled me as I walked by with a sleeping infant strapped to my chest.

You guys are into MILFs? That's so edgy of you! But wait, would it change things if I told you this baby isn't actually mine? I'm just helping out a friend while she works tonight. How do you feel about babysitters? BILFs, if you will. Hey, maybe me, this sleeping angelic form in my arms, and the four of you could all start a babysitter's club together! We'll post flyers, have meetings in my mom's basement, and be the subjects of a series of young adult novels with fuchsia and teal covers! Oh, is that not what you had in mind? No, it's cool, I get it. You're realists about childcare. It's diaper duty and boiling silicone nipples that really turn you on, isn't it? Wow, I really lucked out tonight. Let's all go back to my place and fold nappies while we discuss how society's pigeonholing of women into either sainted mothers or insatiable vamps is so 1994. Obvi, the modern girl can totes be both at the same time! Oh, yeah, def bring your cooler of Pabst.

To the Dating App Guy

A prose poem to the online dating guy who sends women effusively complimentary messages and then, when they don't respond, promptly calls them the c-word.

First, you sounded the depths of my soul through the shallow, imperfect instrument of my OkCupid profile. You knew without knowing that I "seem genuine" and "like I like to have a good time." You knew me better than I know myself. And then. Your sense of righteous justice. Someday, that raw, Cro-Magnon aggression will fend off my immigrant rapist or keep the government fascists from coming to our homestead and taking our guns while I gather our weeping children around the hem of my skirt and pull my bonnet over my rolling doe eyes. And yet. Unfairly. I will never know the comfort of being pressed against your wide, manly chest because I don't want to get coffee with you because I'm a little afraid of you because you called me the c-word online.

You seem cool...
u there?
whatever cunt

I like watching u...
nice work
Welcome sexy
U 2 good 2 answer?
I know u single freak!

To the Stationery Connoisseur

A prose poem to the office guy who leaves his colleagues opaquely suggestive Post-its.

Finally. Finally! A man who appreciates office supplies as much as I do. Baby, you don't have to have clear or coherent messaging as long as the delivery is so tidy, so organized, so administratively sound. Let's hit Staples together. I've got coupons. I want to kiss you under the fluorescent lights of Aisle 7. That's right: the ink and toner aisle, daddy. I want to take you home, along with several reams of bright white 8-½" x 11" laser paper for us to roll around on. I'll come out of the bathroom wearing nothing but a negligee constructed entirely of those file folders with the color-coded tabs. Let me highlight every line and ridge of your body. No, literally. Let me draw on you with a neon green marker. I will run my tongue along your edges, the way I don't have to lick those self-adhesive envelopes with the peel-away sticky strip. I will file you; I will declutter you; I will alphabetize, tabulate, codify, and index you. Honey. Let's get clerical.

To the Coffee Shop Angel

A prose poem to my early morning visitation, my a.m. angel—at last, you've come to save me.

It was 7 a.m. and we'd only just opened for business. My unwashed hair was in a messy bun—universal hairstyle of the barista—and my eyes were still crusted with sleep. You appeared like a vision. A vision that followed me around the coffee shop as I slapped yesterday's detritus off the tables with a wet, gray rag. You wanted to know if I'd worked here long—just long enough to have lost all faith in the humanity of morning commuters. You wanted to know if I was a coffee drinker myself—yes, in quantities carefully calibrated to raise the blood pressure in my ears enough to drown out the chorus of woe that is drudgery for tips at dawn. And then, a surprise question. You wanted to know if I believe in heaven on earth. Absolutely, I do. How could I not? Look around you, my sweet. Behold the clouds parting to pour wisps of golden light over the laminate table tops. Behold the soft pastels and lipstick stains of the paper cups overfilling the garbage can and tumbling to the sticky floor in elegant waves. Behold the clientele, in their droopy business casual and cell phone belt holsters, looking for all the world like the six-winged seraphim circling the throne of God. I do believe in heaven on earth, and I believe that you are my Gabriel come to share the message that the resplendent gates of that heaven on earth are flung open wide for me, and inside? Is a coffee shop. Wrap me in your whiter than white robes, Gabriel, and transport me to that celestial plane that I had no idea I've been laboring in all along, for $7.25 an hour, at 7 a.m., on a Wednesday, in a coffee shop in Madison, Wisconsin.

Menelaus and the Fake Helen

Menelaus's hoary beard is stained red with Trojan blood. Lo, how he sits grieving at the prow of the flagship of a thousand ships, the craggy furrows of his brow deepened with the loss of his brethren, of Patroclus, of dishonored Ajax brought low by his own hand, of even the mighty Achilles. His powerful shoulders bend under the weight of a ten years' war.

Nearby, his wife Helen is moodily gazing at the horizon, smoking a jay.

"Wife." Menelaus's voice rebounds in the cavern of his broad bosom. There is no head aboard that does not turn at the commanding sound. No head but Helen's.

"Cast your eyes upon me, wife," Menelaus booms.

Languidly, Helen extends a bare, bronzed leg. She spreads her toes wide as she stretches the graceful arch of her sandaled foot. Her toenails are painted turquoise with sassy little pearls of glitter at the tips. Very slowly, as if moving through a miasma, she turns her face from distant Sparta toward her husband. Her jaw is as sharp as a blade, her cheekbones impossibly high, like Gisele Bündchen's.

"Dragging me away by the hair was kind of overdramatic, honey," she says. A gentle trail of smoke escapes over the plump, moist mound at the center of her lower lip. Nearby, a brigadier squeezes the guardrail on the starboard side to stay upright. He dipped the point of his spear in the hearts of 491 Trojan cavalrymen, but his constitution is jellied by this small woman.

"I have told you, wife," Menelaus thunders, "that I was sorry for that. But you crack my heart. I have lost all for you. So many men have lost all for you. My brother, Agamemnon, Idomeneus of Crete, Odysseus, so many dropped all to honor the oath of Tyndareus and sail for your virtue, and you, woman, you turn your pale, cold eyes upon the wine-dark sea and do not grace me, your husband, with your thanks, your charms, the treasures of your lap."

"I didn't ask you to come to Troy." Helen takes a long drag on the joint, arching her back and lifting her chin as she does so, exposing her slender, tapering throat to the salt air. A breeze plays through the chiton pleats at her breast so that her cleavage peeps out and retreats again. The bosun, watching her from behind the foremast, lifts a hand to his beard to wipe away a thin strand of drool. "I told you a million times you were fighting for nothing."

Menelaus slams his leather-gauntleted fist down upon his own knee. The blow lands heavily, Menelaus cringes, and Helen smirks.

"You dishonor me, woman," Menelaus roars. "Trojan soil is heavy with Achaean blood. I saw the spears of Euphorbus and Hector buried in the bowels of young Patroclus. I defended his lifeless body with my own. As a cow stands lowing over her first calf, even so did I bestride him." Here the supreme commander's great heart fails him, the sonorous vibrations of his voice die in his lungs. He drops his chin against his tarnished breastplate and weeps.

Helen flicks her jay into the sea. "I don't know how to say this to you any clearer. I'm an idea. I'm an idea in your head. And in Paris's too. I don't exist."

"Even mighty Achilles fell," Menelaus sobs. "The dashed infant brains of Astyanax cannot avenge so great a man."

Helen heaves a sigh, rolls her eyes dramatically into her lashes, long and gently curled like the spread wings of a swan. She stands, and as she does, the folds of her chiton tumble over the swell of her hips. She stretches and yawns, lifting the orbs of her breasts to the light.

A deckhand makes a small, strangled cry, then freezes, his face taut and red, his eyes two enormous, staring discuses. He has come in his pants.

"Seaman," Menelaus murmurs flatly, "get below deck."

The boy scuttles toward the galley ladder, clutching miserably at his crotch.

Menelaus turns to Helen, every molecule of his colossal body drooping with defeat. "I sacked Troy for you," he says.

Helen claps her hands in his face. "I'm an eidolon, you obtuse old fool," she says. "I," she continues, punctuating the word with another clap. "Am." She claps again, the delicacy of her fingers belying their cunning. "Literally." Another clap. "Made." Clap. "Of clouds."

Clap.

Menelaus crumples. Something deep in his interior gives way, and the integrity of the king's citadel-like frame compromises. He folds in on himself. His hands are barely swift enough to catch his heavy head.

Helen is, indeed, made of clouds. Her sandaled feet have already blurred, a kind of wispy hollowness is traveling gently up her calves. Her face, so achingly perfect, is serene, almost expressionless but for the shadow of a smile at the corners of her supple mouth.

Just as her shapely thighs are beginning to disappear, resolving themselves into a shimmering dew and then to thin air, Castor and Polydeuces, her twin brothers and sons of Zeus, come bounding up from the galley, looking for all the world like duplicated Ashton Kutchers.

Castor's emo bangs sweep coyly over his fine brow, and Polydeuces is shouldering a video camera. As Helen's torso turns into vapor, Polydeuces presses the lens into Menelaus's face.

"You have been punk'd!" Castor crows gleefully. Helen's smile is yielding to nothingness. Castor nudges a microphone into Menelaus's face beside the camera lens.

"How does it feel, bro?"

The ship lists sickly to and fro. Helen disappears. Menelaus lifts his eyes to the heavy clouds and wails.

To the Flapper

A prose poem to the man who flapped his cock and balls at me from a dark driveway off 16th Street when I was twenty-two and newly transplanted, wide-eyed and filled with hope, to the big city.

The thought never crossed my mind that I might see a stranger's cock and balls that night. I was shaky, self-conscious, moonishly in love with a boy who had said more than once that it wasn't gonna happen. I was broke, I was gigging, I was thrumming with ready plans. I was getting over a cold. I was in my own mind, I was roiling with everything and nothing—a vessel waiting, as it would happen, for you. And so, caught up in my own little self, unaware of my own blissful ignorance of your cock and balls, I was underprepared when you called to me from your place in the shadows with soft, wet kissing sounds. "Aha! There must be a man in that darkness preparing to give me a look at his cock and balls" was not, as chance would have it, my first thought. Instead, my wee uninitiated understanding offered the following: "It is spring and it is warm and it is evening, and I am hearing a kissing sound. There must be a couple in love, bidding each other goodnight in some private corner off this broad regal avenue in our nation's capital." Imagine then, my consternation when I turned toward the sound and saw not a two but a one. A one with lips puckered, making kissy noises at me. A one with pants open and gaping. A one with forefinger and thumb wrapped securely around the base of both shaft and scrotum, the better to flap with, my dear, up and down up and down, in my (northerly) direction. I was (regrettably) transfixed. Regrettably, I say, but not altogether unjustifiably. A mind that expects to see a scene of sweet romance and is met instead with a triad of cock and balls flapping up and down can be forgiven a temporary lag between stimulus and response. The moment expanded. The moment ended. I turned away. Ah, the sheer limitlessness of the human condition, with its attendant trials and foibles and anguishes and proclivities to flapping complete sets of genitalia at young and naive passers-by in the springtime. You, my unknown suitor, almost gentle in your need for my notice, standing in the silent vulnerability of your offer. "This is me. Here I am." Flap, flap. Flap, flap.

To the Followed

A prose poem to the woman alone who crosses the street when I am walking behind her after dark.

I don't know what makes you think I could be violent. I'm not. I've never even been in a physical altercation with a man, let alone a woman. My greatest pleasure in life is lying in bed after cooking myself a meal of fresh, sautéed vegetables with a dark, earthy Cabernet and reading Flaubert. Sometimes in the original French, if I have the focus for it. I love the opera. When my dog—who is impossibly fluffy and joyful, her name is Abigail—when my dog Abigail poops on the linoleum, then knocks over the kitchen trash can so she can extract and eat a lemon rind, then throws up the lemon rind next to her poop, I tell her "no" gently, with my words, and put her in her crate so she can calm down. She's my best friend. I majored in Sociology, and I love my grandmother. I really love my grandmother. Sometimes I go over to her apartment with leftover sautéed vegetables and Cabernet, and we laugh about the stupid things my dad did when he was a teenager. I am not the kind of man who hurts women, and it hurts me that you think I could be when all you know about me is the sound of my footsteps as we are both walking alone on a deserted urban street after dark. I wish you knew who I really am. I wish you would consider this from my perspective.

To the Guy in the Comment Thread

A prose poem to Matthew, the Facebook commenter who suggests that women post pretty selfies rather than engage in politics.

Oh, Matthew, you make me nostalgic for a simpler time. A time before women felt such pressure to keep our social media presence curated with memes about red wine, pyramid schemes selling lip balms, misspellings of "your" and "you're," and selfies. A time before men felt such pressure to keep their social media presence curated with advice to women about how to keep our social media presence curated. The twenty-first century is just too scary and complicated, you know? There's all this shattered glass ceiling everywhere! Seriously, a girl could chip a nail. Do you wanna get out of here? Back to when things were easy and great again? How about 1919? I'll wear a girdle for you, and you'll sign documents for me. I'll set my hair with hot irons, and you'll own property. I'll be too pretty to think, and you'll cast one ballot for the both of us. Come with me, Matthew. Our buggy's waiting.

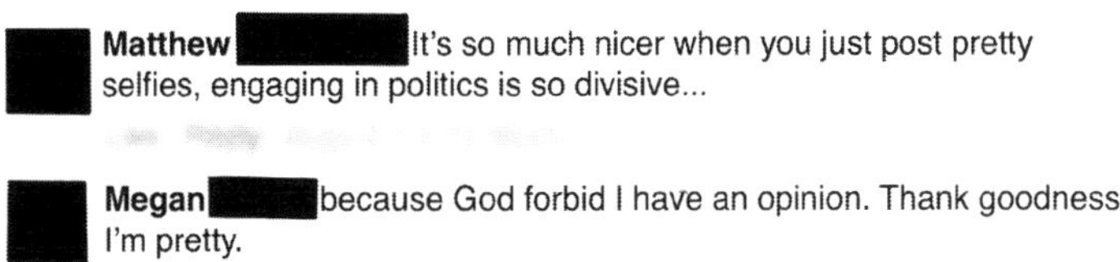

To the Metro Maker-Over

A prose poem to the guy who stands outside the Metro telling women, "You're prettier when you smile."

Sorry, pardon me, what? I'm prettier when I smile? Oh my god, is this a woman-on-the-street makeover? Are you with *Glamour* or *Cosmo* or something? Oh my god, this is so exciting. I never win anything! So, I'm prettier when I smile? Let's try it. I'm smiling. What do you think? Better? On a scale of one to ten, how much improved? Wait, you should probably rate me before the smile and then after the smile so we can calculate the differential more scientifically or whatever. When will I be in the magazine? Is this all there is for my "before" and "after"? Just not smiling and then smiling? Because typically these makeover pieces involve, like, at least one new outfit and then maybe a haircut. Do you do hair? I was thinking maybe an angled bob, but that might be too severe. I don't know, you're the expert. Maybe lowlights? Where are you going?

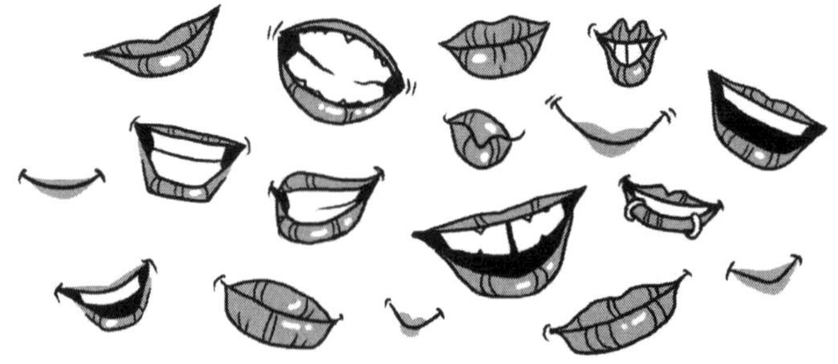

A Nursery Rhyme for Girls Online

One and two
Veiny and blue
Two and three
Knobby like knees
Three and four
Here's some more
Four and five
Is that . . . hives?
Five and six
Dick pics!
Nothing but dick pics!

The cell phone pings
And—this one's got a ring!
Nine and ten
Some of them bend
Fifteen, sixteen
Nonconsensual sexting!
Thirty-seven, thirty-eight
Shaft *and* taint
Forty-nine, fifty
Nifty!
We're drowning in stiffies!

Loose and freckled
Short and wrinkled
Thick and hairy
This one's just scary!
Why did no one tell us?
We're in a phallus palace!
We hoped you'd play nice
Now we're paying the price
Every time we log on:
Schlongs!
A whole lotta schlongs!

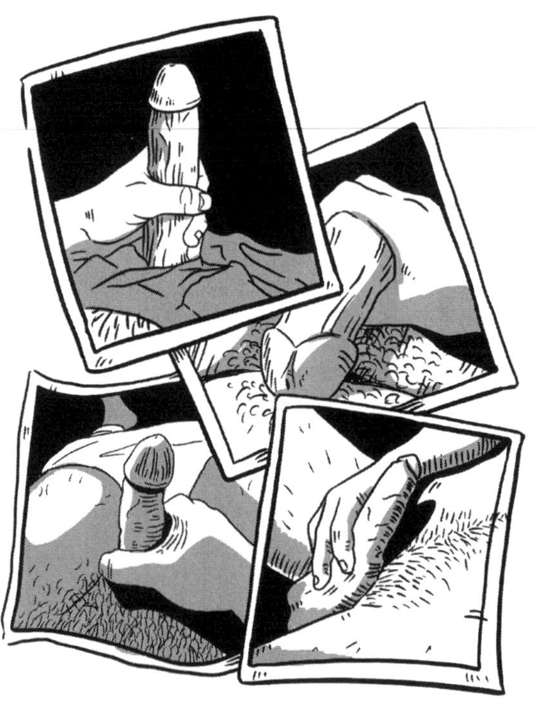

To the Gender Studies Majors

A prose poem to a carful of fragile masculinity.

Maleness and femaleness are, of course, a complex convergence of biology and mores, DNA expression—and social expression. Who is to tell us what makes a woman and what makes a man? Plato's Symposium? The Kinsey Institute? RuPaul's Drag Race? The North Carolina General Assembly? Or, perhaps, the question is best left to you, four bros cruising campus at night. As I walked home after dark, you pulled up alongside me and let loose the standard guy-on-girl litany: the whistles, the hoots, the "Hey, baby's." Gender exists on a Slip 'N Slide of a continuum, but that night, you were so very firmly on the "male" side, the "puff and bluster" side, the "look at us mightily swinging our giant dicks" side. And how badly you wanted me to know my place in relation to yours. So it was a bit perplexing when, in response to my silence, you revved the engine and peeled away, tossing a final rejoinder out the window into your wake: "You look like a man, bitch." In a single sentence, you brought our culture's deepest discomforts into sharp relief. I could dissect that one sentence for a thousand poems and never come out the other side. One moment my femininity attracts your attention. The next, you rebuke me for masculinity. I was brazen enough to be a woman in public, so you shame me for mannishness. Not to mention, of course, the paralyzing cognitive dissonance of those two opposing epithets in one breath, *man* and *bitch*. And further still, the self-incriminating homophobia of four bros caught catcalling a girl who, in their own estimation, looks like a man. We could fall into the rabbit hole of that one sentence—"You look like a man, bitch"—for an eternity. In fact, a decade later, I am still falling. Just me and you . . . a carful of fragility . . . tumbling, plummeting, frozen forever in perpetual free fall through the abyss.

To the Good Husband

A prose poem to the man who offered this passing positive affirmation: "You would make a good wife. I like big women."

There's a saying: Every cap has its bottle. How lucky, how astonishingly, breathtakingly lucky we are, my one true love, that we've found each other. A bottle and its cap. You think big women make good wives? What a stunning coincidence! I think idiots make good husbands. Marry me. Be my only. I'll be an independent, free-thinking, self-actualized woman; you'll sit on the La-Z-Boy mouth breathing. I'll be surrounded by loving, supportive, mutually inspiring friendships; you'll stare out the car window and read the billboards out loud in a monotone. I'll continue to advance in my career, garnering respect and feeling both fulfilled and challenged; you'll gape slack-jawed at your browser, refreshing the same page of college football stats again . . . and again . . . and just . . . one . . . more . . . time. You singular being. You snowflake. You cap to my bottle. You complete me.

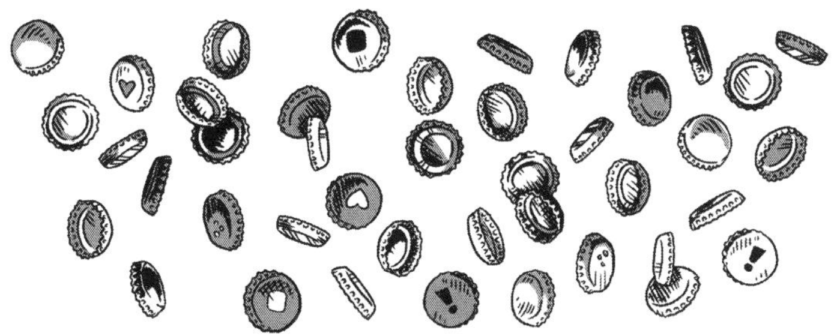

To My Walking Companion

A prose poem to the stranger who is holding my hand.

The English word "liminal" means *in an in-between or transitional state*, and it comes from the Latin word "limen," which means *threshold.* So there is a moment when you are on one side of a door and a moment when you are on the other—and in between, you are crossing over. You are *within* the threshold. That's where the magic happens. What I'm trying to explain is that there was a moment when I was walking along the canal trail alone, watching the ducks, contemplating the clouds, listening to *This American Life*. And then there was a moment when I was walking with you, and you were holding my hand. And in between, there was a crossing over. Or, at least, I think there was. There must have been. There must have been a liminal space in which you said to yourself, "Here is a woman I do not know, have never spoken to in my life, who is alone on a trail and does not notice me approaching because she is wearing earbuds. What I will do now is thread my fingers through hers, as if we did know each other. As if we were lovers." You must have said this to yourself, my enigma, my lover-who-is-not-my-lover, my known and yet unknown, my stranger who is also, evidently, holding my hand. You must have said this to yourself, somewhere in the liminality, because now, here we are, having crossed over, together, entwined. And a new liminal space opens on a narrow path between the canal and a thick growth of trees. After you chose to take my hand. Before I know where you will lead me.

Devil's Advocate

Transcript of Proceedings of the Superior Court of the Sixth Circle of Hell
The Matter Before the Court: Literally No One Asked, But Just for Argument's Sake
Date/Time: Three Beers In

Bailiff: All rise. The Superior Court is now in session. Judge Satan presiding. Please be seated.

Judge Satan: Good evening, gentlemen and lady. Calling the case of the People of Hell versus Some Exhausted Lady Who Doesn't Know How She Got Into This Conversation. I'll be hearing arguments from my personal advocate and from the lady, if she can get a word in edgewise. Are both sides ready?

Lady: Sorry, who are you? What is this?

Devil's Advocate: Born ready, Your Honor.

Judge Satan: Proceed.

Lady: Sorry, I don't know how I ended up in this conversation, I just stopped in for a quick beer after work, and I—

Judge Satan: *(gavel strike)* You'll have your chance, lady. Your opening argument, please, Counsel for Hell.

Devil's Advocate: Your Honor and lady, over the course of the next three unrelenting hours, I plan to submit a litany of evidence clearly and incontrovertibly showing that the lady here is getting worked up over nothing. Case in point: When Louis CK masturbated in front of two lady comics without their consent, those ladies are reported to have started laughing, indicating that it was all definitely no big deal.

Lady: Oh, this is about Louis CK? I mean, laughter is a proven trauma response, not to mention that it's the currency of comedy culture, so maybe they just didn't know what the fuck else to do? But if you're worried you're a bad person because you still laugh at his jokes, I mean look, sometimes I do too—

Judge Satan: *(gavel strike)* The Defendant will maintain decorum in these proceedings.

Lady: Sorry? I thought we were just shooting the shit here, for the sake of argument?

Devil's Advocate: Yeah, but interrupting is rude. Another beer, please, Your Honor?

Judge Satan: Bailiff. Get the man a beer.

Devil's Advocate: Thank you, Your Honor. With regard to Monica Lewinsky, she's on the record telling Linda Tripp that she was in love with him, so—

Lady: She was a twenty-two-year-old intern, and he was the President of the United States.

Devil's Advocate: Are you saying an adult woman is unable to consent? Seems pretty infantilizing. Who's the feminist now?

Lady: What? Look, confiding in a much older and trusted colleague is hardly going "on the record"—

Devil's Advocate: The recordings were within the bounds of the law.

Lady: Um, objection? Your Honor, *were* they, though?

Judge Satan: Overruled. Nitpicking.

Lady: Your Honor, can I get another drink?

Judge Satan: Are you sure that's a good idea, lady?

Lady: . . .

Devil's Advocate: It seems to me like Grace just had a bad date.

Lady: Oh god, not this.

Devil's Advocate: I mean, I think she's got an axe to grind because she's never been treated well before.

Lady: That literally makes no sense. She knew how she wanted to be treated, which was not how Aziz Ansari treated her, so she advocated for herself.

Devil's Advocate: Maybe she's just never been fucked well.

Lady: Your Honor, can I get the check?

Judge Satan: Finish what you started.

Lady: I didn't start this.

Devil's Advocate: What I don't understand is, if she was blackout drunk and doesn't even remember what happened, why is it worth ruining Brock Turner's career over?

Judge Satan: Lady, are you crying?

Devil's Advocate: There's no gender pay gap if you correct for the amount of time women take off to have kids. If girls are on apps because they're DTF, how am I supposed to know they don't want a pic of my nuts? Also, why doesn't she just leave him?

Lady: I . . . okay. Sure. Fine. Can I go home now?

Judge Satan: *(gavel strike)* In the matter before us, the Court finds that ladies be crazy. Adjourned.

Devil's Advocate: Another beer! Hey lady, want another? Lady?

To the Thinker

A prose poem to the 2 a.m. philosopher, reclining on the couch with his baggie of edibles and his probing questions.

"Why aren't women funny?" You ask me thoughtfully, your brows working under the weight of the puzzle. I have to tell you, my sweet interlocutor, it's a mystery. A deep, deep mystery. Like the origin of the universe, the quantum nature of everything, what God eats, and how? This brainteaser you've struck upon, in the black of night and the shallows of human understanding . . . baby, it's a tough one. It's a chicken-or-egg kind of tricky one, a what-is-consciousness kind of sticky wicket. A possibility comes to me. Just a thought. A hunch, no big deal. A shot in the dark, sorry if it's stupid. "I think I'm funny," I offer. Oh no. Now I've done it. Now we're well and truly lost, my sophist. I can see my reflection in your pupils and yours in mine, ricocheting ad infinitum, our eyes wide and staring, the doors of knowledge opening and opening and opening into the nothingness between us. How do I unspeak what I've said? How can I unpluck this bitter fruit? Now there's no going back. We either have to admit out loud that I'm wrong, I'm not funny . . . or that you weren't thinking of me and the myriad times I've made us both howl until the tears ran from our eyes and our sides heaved with aching peals of unfettered hilarity. You weren't thinking of me as a real woman at all. I'm not a woman, I'm your friend. Take us back, oh take us back to the gentleness of our ignorance! "I recant," I want to call into this rift between us. We can both be safe again, we can claw our way back to the solid ground of Eden, where all is clear and we know who we are and who we must be, we're going to be okay, we are, we can be, I can feel it—"I don't count!" I want to scream. "Only *fuckable* women aren't funny!"

To the Parking Helper

A prose poem to the gentleman who stops to offer women unsolicited parallel parking instructions.

I first glimpsed you on the sidewalk as I angled my car backward into a smallish but not impossible spot on 7th Street. In my periphery, a flash of motion. Our eyes met. You held your fists in perfect isolation, giving me to understand that you were gripping an invisible steering wheel. “Turn the wheel right,” you mouthed, and your hands danced along to illustrate. I don’t think you know how adorable you look, standing there on the sidewalk gesticulating. I want to smush your ruddy helpful cheeks—just smush ‘em—and tousle your graying, competent hair. What would I have done without your authority on this subject? What will I do wrong next without your guidance? Be my life partner, sail with me on this voyage as my sweet, mute semaphorist, capably signaling me through all of life’s narrow passages.

To the Blizzard Opportunist

A prose poem to the construction worker who "just wanted to talk" while I was digging my car out of a Kilimanjaro of snow.

Huh? What? Oh . . . Hi there. *shovel* *grunt* *pause* I'm . . . fine . . . How are you? Did you . . . need something? *shovel* Well . . . as you can see . . . I am . . . shoveling . . . a literal blizzard off of my car . . . while streams of cold sweat . . . run down my face and into my scarf . . . so . . . no, thanks, I don't really feel like . . . having a conversation. *gasp* *shovel* *pause* How am I doing? I thought we covered that ground already. *scoop scoop* My cheeks . . . are chapped and I'm . . . standing . . . up to my thighs in snow . . . so, to answer your question . . . I'm completely bewildered that I'm getting hit on, thanks. *shovel* *heave* *pant* Look, this is . . . flattering . . . but . . . I kind of need my . . . lung power right now, so . . . *shovel* . . . *shovel* . . . *gasp* . . . *shovel* . . . Are you still here?

To the Street Pisser

A prose poem to the guy who whipped it out and let flow a stream of urine in the middle of the street, right in front of me.

It was just after midnight, on a deserted side street off Connecticut Avenue. The lamplight had turned the asphalt, and the night around it, a sort of maudlin *Casablanca* blue-gray. I parked my car, stepped out, and began to cross the silent street. And just then, you stepped out too. We met like two duelists in an old Western. The street was empty but for us. The air was pregnant. And you, my surprising one, were quick on the draw. You whipped it out and pissed in the street, legs confidently akimbo, shoulders back, gaze steady. More surprising, even, than the sheer audacity of pissing in the street for an audience of one is that you were wearing a sweater vest and loafers. My darling, my heart, my god among men . . . you were wearing a sweater vest and loafers. And you were pissing in the street. Who are you? It's entirely possible that you just didn't see me there, twenty feet away, on an otherwise lonely and lamplit street. But I hope not. I hope that the memory I cling to is a true one: that our eyes met over the rivulet of pee between us and that for a moment, however briefly, we were one.

To My Empty Gas Tank

A prose poem to two yokels lurking weirdly in an SUV at the edge of a gas station parking lot at night.

Picture the scene, my sweet ones. You: two dudes enjoying a Thursday night sitting in a parked vehicle in the shadows of a deserted location. Me: a woman alone at 11 p.m. just trying to fill my tank and get home. You: leaning out of your SUV window and into the darkness, calling me "baby." Me: so utterly skeeved that I peeled out of there with only 3.124 gallons of gas when what I really needed was a full tank because I've got a busy schedule, dammit, and not a moment to stop a second time to fill the remaining 11.876 gallons. Your technique is so flawless. Park in an odd and boring spot, let darkness fall, and wait for the ladies to roll in. When they arrive, cause them thorough inconvenience. If I hadn't been in such a silly rush to drive away—my gas cap still unscrewed and dangling—the three of us might really have had a future together. We could park in that creepy little nook under the overpass, listening to Metallica and passing around a bag of Bugles and a twenty-ounce Mountain Dew. Then, at random intervals, when I least expect it, you could keep me on my toes by throwing a wrench in my agenda. Come on, you sexy beasts. Interrupt me when I'm in the middle of buying my groceries so that

I have to spend the whole week without my favorite blend of Greek yogurt and honey. Distract me while I'm paying the bills so that the Verizon check goes unsigned and my cable is unceremoniously canceled. Stop my doctor mid-Pap smear. No, no, it's okay, I'll just reschedule. Anything for you, my two bold, beautiful, lurking yokel darlings.

To the Carrier

A prose poem to the man who offered to carry my bag—and me—as I walked by with my groceries.

Really? Because that would be so helpful! It's like ninety degrees out here, and I've got so many frozen dinners from Trader Joe's in this bag. How do you wanna do this? Maybe you carry the bag, and then I'll just jump on your back—hold still got it got it lemme just move my foot. Okay. So my car is that way. This is so nice of you. Shit shit shit my cantaloupe is about to fall out of the bag look out oh fuck. Leave it. No just leave it there's a van coming shit there goes my cantaloupe. It's so nice of you to do this on such a hot day. Look . . . our perspiration is combining to form a sort of patina, a glistening wet chrysalis inside of which, I know, our hearts will merge and sprout wings.

LIFE
SALT

To the Admirer of Poop Scooping

A prose poem to the man who honked at me while I was bent over to scoop my dog's poop.

I imagine myself from your perspective: a flash of derriere as you speed by on a lazy Sunday morning. I can't disagree with your sense of aesthetics. The female form, after all, is at its best in the attitude required for poop scooping. Knees gently bent in casual arabesque, rump rising and round against the morning sky. You appreciate a finely drawn scene when you see one: the delicate art of womanhood so tantalizingly juxtaposed against the mundanity of Sunday morning dog shit. The sacred and the profane. I'm awed by your intuitive grasp of the sublime in everyday existence. You and I are the kind of couple who might one day read aloud to one another from the verses of Coleridge while passing back and forth a handle of Skol, gagging as it goes down like lighter fluid. We're the kind of highbrow raunch artists who could find a nook for a quickie in St. Peter's. Let's go bowling in evening attire. Let's waltz barefoot in a field of cow patties. You say you like the look of my bum while I'm sluicing dog poo off the dew-wet grass? I say you're my kindred spirit.

REALLY?

To the Strong, Silent Type

A prose poem to the gentleman who makes "nice rack" gestures at women as they pass.

You and I, we don't need words. Words are for those shallow, quotidian couples who love like the needle of a record player rebounding endlessly over the same groove. "How was your day?" "I'm swinging by Whole Foods, what do we need?" "Don't use the upstairs toilet; it's backed up again." You and I, we transcend. We don't speak—we meld. And so, when you hover your cupped hands a few inches over your chest and pump your fingers, in and out, in and out . . . I know. You don't need words to tell me I've got a nice rack because you and I, baby, we speak a subtler language. We speak the language of lovers' bodies moving in such harmony that even the most delicate honking of a hand is enough to let me know that I am understood. I am seen. I am heard.

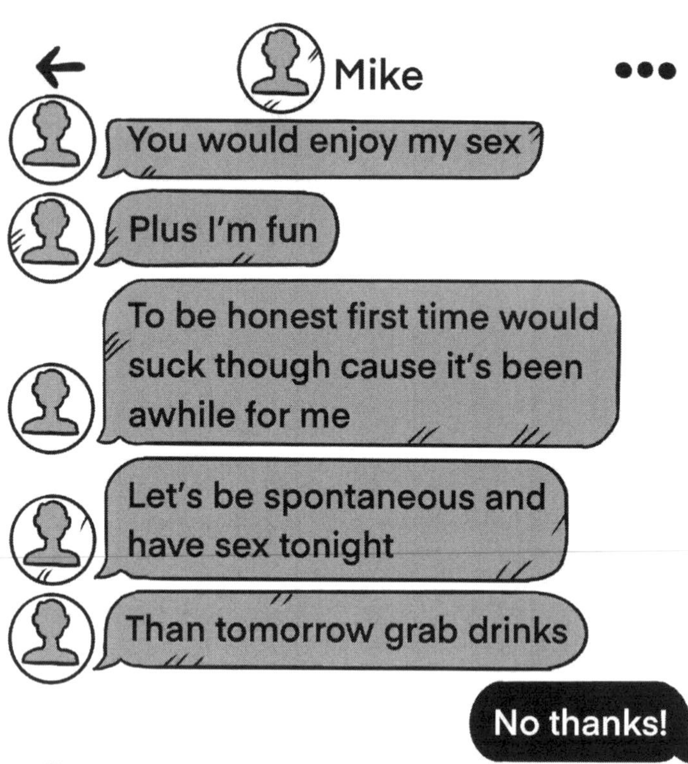
Mike
You would enjoy my sex
Plus I'm fun
To be honest first time would suck though cause it's been awhile for me
Let's be spontaneous and have sex tonight
Than tomorrow grab drinks
No thanks!
Y not if I may Ask

To the Tinder Propositioner

A prose poem to Mike, who wants to know, if he may Ask, Y Tinder lady says no.

Message one? Bold and brash. Declarative. Message two? Bolder. Brasher. Unadulterated confidence. You have something to offer, and you know I want it. But Message three? A sharp left turn. Like a rosebud unfurling in the slow warmth of early dawn, you delicately peel back those dauntless outer petals to reveal a soft, vulnerable center. "To be honest," you say. To be honest. Let's run away together, Honest Mike—let's be a fearlessly unguarded super couple dropping truth bombs on the masses and their lives of quiet obfuscation. Better yet: Let's start a husband-and-wife marketing firm with a bent toward upholding truth in advertising. We'll coach our clients on how to mitigate expectations with catchphrases like "Capable . . . but never above the bar!" and "Decent until proven unsatisfactory." And when our company goes under, we'll file for Chapter 7 bankruptcy and divorce concurrently because, to be honest, we both knew we were never actually cut out for success. Not the first time around, anyway.

To the Birthday Boy

A prose poem of apology to my darling, whom I let down, and on your birthday too.

This morning I rose at dawn, my thoughts filled only with you. That wasn't enough; I see that now. My project on this day, your birthday, an impossible one: to show you how much you mean to me, how very grateful I am that you were born and that you chose me. I can see now, of course, that I was not equal to such a task. You graced the world with your birth, and I? I cooked you Welsh rarebit. It was a paltry offering; that seems obvious now. An anemic idea, to nourish you with the food of your homeland as your love has nourished me. To express in some small, trifling way that home, to me, is wherever you are. Yes, I see now that I fell short. I fell short in my hours-long search for the most authentic, Welsh grandmotherly recipe. I fell short in my special order of cheese, shipped direct across the Atlantic and reserved carefully for me by the rare import grocer. I fell short in my pathetic churning of ale, mustard, and cheese into what I now know was a sad, sad béchamel. Only light of my life, I can see clearly now that when I came to you on the evening of your birthday, bearing the fruits of my poor labor and whispering in my too eager way, "Guess what I have for you?", your guess was the only right one, the thing I should—I see so painfully, exquisitely clearly now—have actually spent the whole day preparing. "Is it a threesome with your best friend?" You, my sweet, wanted sex with me, and also with my best friend, at the same time, for your birthday. And I? Fool that I am. I made you cheese on toast.

To the Bike Pumper

A prose poem to Randall, who knew my bike tire pump for the cry for help that it was.

I was already kneeling, mid-engaged in topping off my bike tire with air, when you came running, vaulting a tree box and neatly sidestepping a labradoodle and her owner to come to my rescue. Yes, Randall. Yes, please, fill my nearly bursting tire with more air. That's my house behind us. Would you come inside, unfold my panties, and then refold them? What? Why? Because I thought this was a game where I complete a task to my own satisfaction and then you redo it for me because I'm a girl. Wait wait wait, if you just crouch down, I'll regurgitate my lunch into your mouth and then you can digest it and poo on my behalf. What's that, Randall? Do my husband and I bike together? You're trying to find out if I'm attached? This is deeply disappointing. I thought you wanted to help me for the sheer altruistic frisson. The sense of community belonging. The human heart-to-heart. I'll poo for myself, then, thank you very much.

To the Nu Beta Beta Bros at Old Ivy

A prose poem to the fraternity brothers of Nu Beta Beta at Old Ivy State College.

Hey, Mom, pull over, it says, "Freshman daughter drop-off." No, I really think this is where I'm supposed to be because who else, if not me, is "ready for a good time" at Old Ivy? I bet they've got Minecraft and a ping-pong table crusted with a year-old veneer of Natty Light and lonely ejaculate. Don't you think there's a brother in there who wants to slip a plaid Urban Outfittered arm around my adolescent waist and walk with me over the rolling campus lawns, confessing to me his minor academic shortcomings (B+ in Close Readings of the Second Sex? I'm sure the professor just didn't get you!) and his humanitarian professional ambitions (community organizer in East LA? You and your enormous heart are a shoo-in, an absolute shoo-in). This is the bro to whom I will whisper, as we spoon precariously on his extra-long dorm-issue twin bed, about losing the family dog so suddenly after we thought the surgery had worked, about that stupid fight with my sister and how neither of us had ever said anything quite so mean ever before, about how my Calc-Based Physics prof is unfair, so completely out of line with that lab write-up deadline. Mom! Mom! Look, it says, "Drop off Mom too!" I know as a professor emeritus happily married to Dad for the last thirty-four years, it's a hard sell, but don't you think you should at least give it some thought?

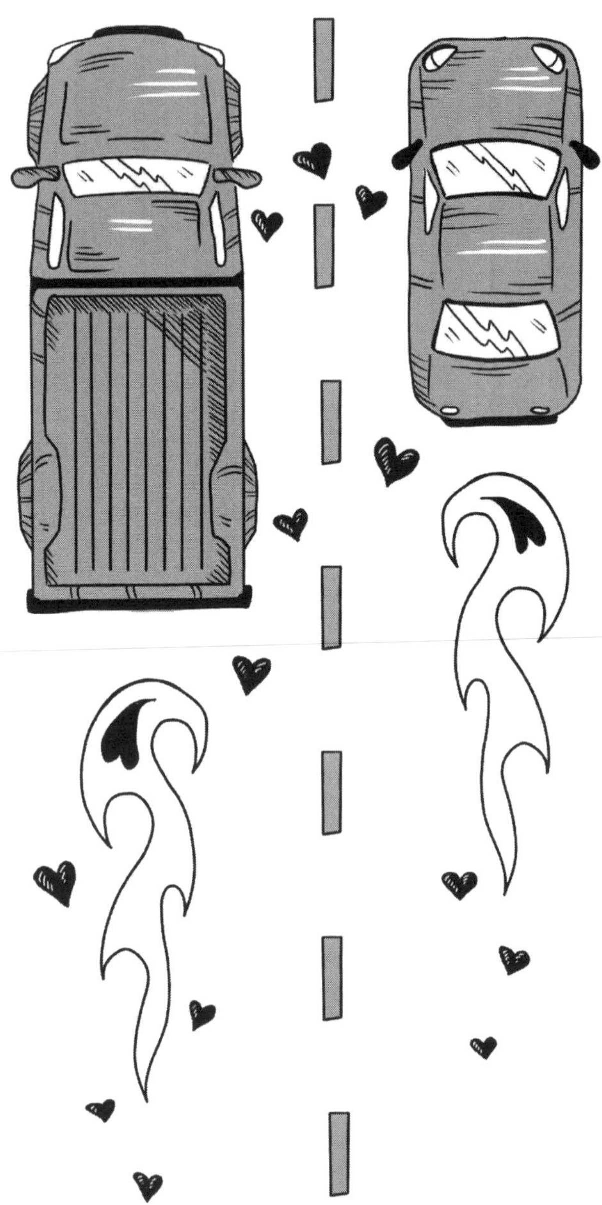

To the Picker-Up in the Pickup

A prose poem to the driver who uses the pickup of his pickup to pick women up.

I passed you innocently enough going eastbound on I-70. One of the greatest tragedies of this life is, after all, that our souls don't always recognize each other instantly, and so, time and again, we pass a kindred spirit in a crowd and never even know that he could have been our dear one. But *you* knew. No sooner had I passed you than you revved the engine of your rusted olive pickup and pulled up alongside my Japanese coupe. For a brief stretch of highway—fifty yards? a hundred?—we were yoked. Two parallel vessels traveling in tandem. Two drag racers on a one-way course to bliss. I imagined telling my girlfriends about our meet-cute. One moment, our tires were on the asphalt, spinning in exquisite unison, and the next, like Canada geese taking wing from a still pool, we were soaring, sailing skyward on the updraft of our love. This is what I imagined. But what actually happened was that you got stuck behind a slow-moving tractor-trailer in the right lane, and I drove on.

Syllabus

Course: *Intro to Femininity*

Department: The Larger Culture

Professors: This course is team-taught by the Chairman of the Department, Your Boss, Your Boyfriends (All of Them), Those Girls (The Ones Who Are Better Than You), Glossy Magazines in the Grocery Checkout Aisle, Your Congressman, Your Gynecologist, God the Father, and Those Three Kinda Scary Preteen Boys Who Hung Out Near Your Locker in Seventh Grade

Office Hours: We have an open-door policy. Please see us with any questions or concerns at any time. We will listen with one eyebrow raised, nodding slowly, asking you to repeat factual statements and/or your description of events as you lived them until you cry and it is clear that this unnecessary meeting is over, or you begin to doubt your own sanity, at which point we will either hit on you or determine that you are not worth hitting on, at which point this unnecessary meeting is over. Also, meetings are by appointment only, and no appointments are currently available.

Course Schedule

Year 1

Assignment:

You will dress in pink and not blue. Bonus points for bows, ribbons, or day-of-the-week barrettes affixed to your wispy infant hair. Points deducted for dinosaurs and heavy farm equipment.

Student Learning Outcomes:

- You are not yet expected to have developed the ability to see color, but your assignment should demonstrate that you have acquired a sense of the immovable parameters of your physical, psychological, intellectual, social, and sexual life.
    - Note: You are not expected to have developed secondary sex characteristics or any awareness of what sex is or the ability to speak the word "sex."
- There is no grade consequence should your barrettes uproot your wispy infant hair and fall out. This is not your fault and kind of to be expected.

Year 2

Assignment:

You will play with a doll and not a plastic neon-green shark with cartoonishly round eyes and a friendly smile.

Student Learning Outcomes:

- You will be able to sort genderless items by gender with the uncanny foreknowledge of a clairvoyant.
- Example items for sorting: teacups, hammers, bricks, plastic ponies with no genitalia, porcelain saucers, flying saucers, flowers, sticks, all teddy bears except those wearing baseball caps, baseball, cinnamon sugar, cayenne pepper, the term of endearment "sweetheart," the term of endearment "champ."

Year 3

Assignment:

You will receive a Lego set for building a princess palace for Christmas. Every Lego piece will be pale pastel purple. Your brother will receive a Lego set for building the *Starship Enterprise*. Every Lego piece will be a shade of gray.

Student Learning Outcomes:

- This is remedial work. Repeat your study of the above categories.
- Further example categories: adrenaline and cortisol, any human emotion except aggression, the nursing profession, the law.

Year 4

Assignment:

The boys will run shirtless through the sprinkler on the front lawn, and you will pull off your shirt too and run through after them. You will be yelled at by three neighborhood moms at the same time.

Student Learning Outcomes:

- You will develop a deep, amygdala-level understanding that there is something shameful about your body and that it is your fault.
  - Note: You do not now or really ever need to know *why* it is shameful, just that it *is* shameful.
  - Also note: You are still not expected to have developed secondary sex characteristics. You should absolutely know, however, about sex categories, cf. Years 2 and 3.

Year 5

Assignment:

You will eat off a placemat with all the Presidents of the United States on it. Your dad will ask you if you are going to be president when you grow up. You will look down at the mustachioed and solemn faces gazing back up at you and shake your head.

Student Learning Outcomes:

- You will develop the ability to identify patterns and your place within them.

Year 6

Assignment:

You will compose an anonymous love letter to your first crush and leave it in his cubby at school. He will promptly hand it over to the teacher, who will ask every girl in class individually if she wrote the letter. You will cross your fingers behind your back and say you did not.

Student Learning Outcomes:

- Girls do not make the first move.
- Your feelings are embarrassing to everyone who has to witness them, and acting on them is right out.
- Duplicity, from here on out, is a necessary practical skill.

Year 7

Assignment:

You will earn a Fashion badge in Brownies by completing an activity to determine "what your colors are."

Student Learning Outcomes:

- You will identify the best color palette for your skin tone and hair texture.
- The uses and applications of this knowledge for a seven-year-old are patently obvious. If they are not, complete remedial study Years 1 through 3.

- Bonus learning: the Girl Scout pledge begins with, "On my honor, I will try." The Boy Scout pledge begins with, "On my honor, I will."
    - Integrate into all your practices that his job is to do, while yours is just to try.

Year 8

Reading List:

Little House on the Prairie
Little Women
Anne of Green Gables
The Secret Garden
A Little Princess

Student Learning Outcomes:

- Domesticity
- Gardens
- Pinafores
- Imagination games!
- Littleness

Year 9

Assignment:

Your consciousness will slip quietly outside your body and come to rest in the far corner of the room, where it can watch you from a safe distance.

Student Learning Outcomes:

- There is nothing to be learned from this beyond basic survival. Repeat this practice regularly for the rest of your life.

Year 10

Assignment:

A boy on the playground will call you fat.

Student Learning Outcomes:

- It is worse to be a girl who is a little fat than to be a boy who is a little shit.

Year 11

Assignment:

On a Girl Scout camping trip, you will ask one of the troop moms for a Band-Aid to cover the nick you gave your knee while shaving. She will say, "God sometimes has little ways of reminding us to be humble when we try to get ahead of our friends." You will not know how to tell her that it was her daughter who gave you her three-week-old razor and told you to shave your gross, hairy legs or you couldn't sleep in her tent.

Student Learning Outcomes:

- Your body is gross.
- So is your vanity.

Year 12

Assignment:

In Health class, surrounded by thirty other awkward middle schoolers, you will learn that there is a word for what happened to you in Year 9 and that it is "rape" and that it is a crime. Your Health teacher will immediately turn off the lights for a short video about drug abuse, so don't worry, no one will see the look on your face.

Student Learning Outcomes:

- This is remedial learning. We probably should have given you this vocabulary in Year 9; we just couldn't imagine that you would need it so soon.

Year 13

Assignment:

Your dad will declare at the Thanksgiving table that he thinks you're going to be a real beauty, and all sixteen guests will turn to look at you and openly assess whether or not they agree. You will have one second to come up with a response that is both graceful and self-deprecatingly witty beyond your years. Should you instead blush and reply with adolescent petulance, the faces of all sixteen guests will register that they think your dad is exaggerating, and they will return to their soup in awkward silence.

Student Learning Outcomes:

- You will develop comprehension of the following broad concepts:
  - Your value
  - Your appearance
  - The equivalence of the two

Year 14

Assignment:

The girls on your club soccer team will mock you viciously for painting your bedroom a pretty rose pink.

Student Learning Outcomes:

- Having learned in prior years to conform unwaveringly to gender markers, you will now begin the subtle and precarious process of simultaneously conforming with and differentiating yourself from "those girls."
- You must, from now on, be the first girl to declare, "Oh my god, I *hate* girls. I get along so much better with guys" in all co-ed conversations. Failure to do this makes you one of "those girls." Which is the worst thing you could be. Obviously.

Year 15

Assignment:

Not wanting to be the odd one out, you will drink two beers and run in your bra and underwear around the cul-de-sac with a group of freshmen at your first high school party. One of the boys will tell everyone to look at your tits, you look like an eight-year-old boy. His erection when he says this will be obvious.

Student Learning Outcomes:

- There will always be something wrong with you.
- You must correct this flaw by doggedly seeking the approval of boys.
- You will not succeed.

Year 16

Assignment:

After ordering fries, a boy you do not know will ask for your number while you are working the cash register at Burger King. Startled by the abrupt non sequitur, you will decline. On his way out the door with his friends and his fries, he will turn and scream, "Ugly fuck!" at you across the crowded restaurant.

Student Learning Outcomes:

- You will understand that it is your responsibility to manage his feelings.
- If you fail at this, his choices are always your fault.

Year 17

Assignment:

Your thirty-something-year-old manager at Old Navy will contrive a reason to drive you around in his 1994 hatchback Honda Civic, complaining about not getting into Dartmouth and offering you detailed play-by-plays of his sexual encounters with his girlfriend, who is also your co-worker at Old Navy. He will watch your facial expressions carefully.

Student Learning Outcomes:

- If Learning Outcomes from Years 13 through 16 are properly integrated, you will feel simultaneous revulsion and a feeling of accomplishment and privilege at being chosen.

Year 17 and a quarter

Assignment:

You will witness Joey's friends telling his girlfriend she smells like fish and laughing in her face. Joey will not intervene.

Student Learning Outcomes:

- Just be glad you aren't Joey's girlfriend.

Year 17 and a half

Assignment:

You will yawn hugely while riding the subway at the end of a very long day. A suit-clad businessman will snidely remark, at a volume intended for both you and all nearby passengers, "Well, *that* was attractive."

Student Learning Outcomes:

- Regardless of your exhaustion or sadness, you must be attractive at all times.
- You are not.

Year 17 and three-quarters

Assignment:

Your first love will call you "emotionally unstable" when you cry while he is dumping you.

Student Learning Outcomes:

- You are a hysteric.
- He might not have dumped you if you were different.
- You can see this most clearly from outside yourself, in the far corner of the room. Stay there. Tell no one of this refuge. Note the myriad ways that you've brought all of this on yourself.

Year 18

FINAL EXAM:

1. Layer your cap and gown over a tight mini dress—not too tight, not too mini—and high heels that you can easily walk across the stage in to collect your diploma but that also accentuate your breasts and buttocks under your cap and gown and also that grandma would approve of. And your boyfriend. But not the weird Social Studies teacher with the mustard stain on his polo, Mr. Carle.

2. Deliver the valedictory address; use a healthy selection of multisyllabic Latinate words and artfully constructed metaphors. Smile while speaking. Don't make the boys feel less-than.
3. Collect your diploma with the appropriate level of deference, confidence, eye contact, palm moisture, poise, sexiness, clever repartee, and winsome humility. Do not look at your feet as you cross the stage, however high your heels may be, and also don't look the principal in the eye; he takes umbrage easily. Suck in your tummy.

GRADING SCHEMA: Pass/Fail

- No one gets a pass.

Trampwise.com
Maison Plage et Soleil

3.5/5 stars: Terrific cake, hold the assault!

If there's one thing the team at Maison Plage et Soleil gets right, it's personal attention! I felt cared for from the moment my tour group arrived. As soon as we stepped into the lobby, I could feel the concierge's eyes following my every move—even when my back was turned! I didn't even have to call down for room service, he appeared at my door pronto with hot jasmine tea and those unblinking eyes. Actually, I would have preferred if he waited for a call, I was just about to shower and I don't really drink tea, so it was awkward, but it's the thought that counts. And he had such stick-to-itiveness! He insisted on laying the tea service for me, which really was going above and beyond because it meant coming all the way into the room and steering the cart into a very narrow cranny between the bed and the balcony doors. I have to admit, that's one thing the Maison Plage et Soleil falls short on: decor. A king-sized canopy bed that takes up most of the room? Methinks the hotel designer doth protest too much! And that reminds me: I will warn future guests that these *fin-de-siècle* buildings aren't well-equipped with means of egress. There's no fire escape off the balcony—but you gotta hand it to them for those adorable ivy-clad trellises! I wish the door to the room weren't in a corner too. One warm body in the doorway, and Bob's your uncle, guess you're a shut-in for the evening! Anyway, that tea service was cute, tiny roses painted around the spout, but pee yew! Jasmine is a strong scent in a small room, especially when you weren't expecting it! Things got a little dicey around tipping protocols—you know, strange girl, foreign land and all! I offered a few coins but I think the *malentendu* arose from the concierge's impression that I owed him? Something about "enticing him since I arrived"? Not sure what that was about, maybe I dropped the ball on some customary exchange around our check-in, maybe bag service? Yikes! Talk about a gaffe! That's when he blocked the door and grabbed my ass, which made me think I must really not understand the bartering system! I considered a quick swing down the trellises, but honestly, my tourism style is more kick-back-and-relax than dive-in-head-first, so I opted instead for a sprint through the corridors. Plush carpets! Crown molding! But watch out for that *fin-de-siècle* narrowness and tricky stairway-to-nowhere design. I gotta say, the whole labyrinth thing feels a little forced. By the time I got to the front desk: there he was! So reassuring to know the employees know the ins and outs of this place like the workings of one of those intricate pocket watches with all the gears and valves this city is so famous for. It's almost scary how quick he moved—talk about at-the-ready.

But just my luck! That no-man-left-behind attentiveness extends to the whole staff, because there was the hotelier at my elbow and at my service! I told him about our little mix-up, and that's when I saw the Maison Plage et Soleil's true colors. This is a never-give-up establishment, travelers. Boy, was he determined to make things right! Tickety boo, before I knew it, I was wedged between that same concierge and the hotelier in a charmingly miniature alcove and the hotelier was demanding the concierge deliver me a personal apology. How debonair! Future guests, if I have one suggestion for the Maison Plage et Soleil—and, really, it's only a small thing—it's that they add some lighting to that alcove. Just a titch. Anyway, from there I thought the whole lost-in-translation episode was surely behind us and all that was ahead was that promised beach and sun. But I was in for another surprise! That sweet hotelier—well, he really outdid himself in the old "Sorry about my employee's whoopsiedaisy" department! The last thing I expected was a party, but that's the first thing I got! Imagine my surprise when that evening I found myself surrounded by all of the hotel's employees—minus, interestingly, the concierge (maybe he takes the day shift)—and my entire tour group (a little bleary-eyed and worse-for-wear, maybe due to the byzantine police reporting and witness statement process in what is for most of us a second language). But the hotelier correctly sniffed out that we were all due for a break in the excitement, and he sure did deliver. That's when the topper came, fellow travelers. You'll never guess what that nice hotelier had in store for us all! He baked me a cake. Himself! Strawberry. My favorite. The icing on the cake was—well, it was the literal icing on the cake. I think the message the hotelier spelled out, in pink buttercream script, sums up my time at Maison Plage et Soleil perfectly. In one simple word. "Welcome."

tl;dr: A few hiccups during my stay, but I'm putting this down for 3.5 stars, would recommend for the cake and personal service, would be 4 if they put up a nice sconce in that alcove.

To the Follower Home

A prose poem to the dude who followed me home in Los Feliz.

I remember the clicking of our footsteps in the gloaming, so perfectly in sync. I sped up, I slowed down, and you matched my pace until I hardly knew where I ended and you began. And then, when I paused at the front door . . . so did you. There were universes in that brief hiccup of silence. God, how I wanted to tumble into the bottomless sea of your eyes. But when I turned to find you, I saw only your knees peeking out from your crouch behind the hedge. Why so shy? I know there can only be one reason for your coy game of Follow the Leader: You are a magnificent lover. So why hide it? Honey, don't be coquettish. You know you're not being fair, out here on the street hawking a bill of goods you don't mean to deliver. Come on out from behind that hedge, you bashful little minx. Let me push you inside the foyer, let me press you tenderly against the bank of silver corrugated mailboxes. Let me give you what you're asking for.

To the Creative Catcaller

A prose poem to the man on H Street who told me my "booty look like it got somethin' to say."

It does. My booty has so much to say, mainly that it longs to become conversant in the language of yours. What tender lovers' symphony might we, together, compose? I'll fart like distant clapping. You, like a rising snare roll. Trumpets naturally come to mind. But also bass oboe. A soupçon of timpani? Low, mournful farts more ache than sound. Quiet, whispered farts peeping demurely from under the duvet. Insistent, honking farts like when you're trying to feed the ducks and you accidentally stir up a gaggle of aggressive geese. The kind of plaintive, mewling farts that make farmhands look up from their bales and ask if the cat has finally delivered her kittens in the barn. Propulsive farts. Sharts. My booty look like it got somethin' to say? So much. So much, sweet lover, and it's all for you.

To the Stardust

A prose poem to the streak of radiant, astonishing stardust that illuminated the blackest of night skies just long enough for me to draw breath.

"Girl, those pants are slammin'!" you flung over your shoulder as you passed. The street was crowded enough, and my mind was jumbled enough, that by the time I organized your words into a sequence—whose pants? *my* pants? slammin'?—you were gone. I'll never know who you are. I'll never even know what you look like beyond a tossing train of ponytail, a flowered skirt hem, a streak of smile vanishing in your magical wake. And you'll never know who I am. You'll never know that as you sailed past, sprinkling manna from your tender heavens, I was standing there on 14th, wrapped in a shroud of heartache, thinking what the fuck, what the fuck, what the fuck am I even doing here? My pants, though. My pants *were* slammin', girl. Fly and silken, a palazzo number, with vertical stripes rising to cup and lift my ass to the sun, an ass so cuppable and liftable that day, only because I was subsisting on a post-loss diet of nothing but black coffee, red wine, and over-easy misery. You didn't know that. You knew only that I was standing still, staring at nothing, and my pants were slammin'. And you told me so. And an étoile of light exploded through the otherwise interminable darkness of that time in my life, and I thought, "Yes. Yes, girl. My pants are slammin'." And I walked on.

Acknowledgments

This collection began as a Tumblr. In 2016, several of the prose poems appeared in slightly different form in *The Establishment* as a weekly series titled "Love Poems to My Catcallers": "To the Trucker," "To the Gender Studies Majors (To the Gender Studies Experts)," "To the Follower Home," "To the Shouter," and "To the Creative Catcaller (To the Derriere Enthusiast)." The multimedia arts company Walterhoope adapted five poems into short films, released in 2018: "To the Shouter," "To the Parking Helper," "To the Tinder Propositioner," "To the Follower Home," and "To the Creative Catcaller." "Menelaus and the Fake Helen" originally appeared in *Defenestration* in August 2022. Robert Lucaciu and Fallen Crooner released a jazz composition of "To the Creative Catcaller" in 2023.

As this project has evolved, I've been bowled over by how many excellent humans have jumped in to lend essential creative support. I owe my enormous thanks to my partner in this endeavor, Sydney Schwindt, whose illustrations complete me. Audrey Bertaux, David Mavricos, and William Vaughan of Walterhoope saw that this writing could come off the page and made it so with short films that make me cry-laugh. Christopher DeWan's editorial insight shaped what was otherwise a hot mess, along with the sharp eyes and wits of Bree Barton, Rana Kay, Kelsey Mesa, and Honora Talbott. And I am wholly and always grateful to and over the moon for my husband Mark and son Arlo, for everything.

Marcus Kyd of Taffety Punk Theatre Company, where I am a company member, has always seen possibilities in this series that I didn't know were there. Taffety Punk is a Washington, DC-based collaborative company of artists who make awesome art in all kinds of media. The Punks' vision and support made this collection possible in book and audiobook form. In particular, the following company members and friends gathered to read early drafts and offered comments that reshaped the whole shebang for the better: Ian Armstrong, Aaron and Renee Beaver, Tonya Beckman, Lise Bruneau, Kathy Cashel, Adrienne Nelson, and Esther Williamson. As we moved toward publication, we were cheered on by M. L. Rio, and Sara Stratton and everyone at Redwood Publishing contributed essential wisdom and expertise. The audiobook production could not have happened without a host of collaborators: Danny Cackley and the good people of Capitol Hill Arts Workshop, and Pete and Judy at Rohan Audio in New York, made space and time to record; Gabra Zackman made engineer introductions; and the Riot Grrrls plus Omar D. Cruz and Dan Crane lent us their badass voices. Many thanks also to Lee Anne Myslewski and Wolf Trap Opera, Mark Anderson and Positive Force DC, and St. Stephen and the Incarnation Episcopal Church. Taffety Punk hosted early readings of the poems, and the District Alliance for Safe Housing, Men Can Stop Rape, and the DC Rape Crisis Center sent representatives. Taffety Punk extends an extra thank you to donors and the DC Commission on the Arts and Humanities, the SHARE Fund, and the Capitol Hill Community Foundation for ongoing support.

Most of all: my gratitude to the women whose stories and radical laughter form the basis of this book.